# Glimpses of Heaven

**Resources by Dave Dravecky**
*Comeback* (with Tim Stafford)
*When You Can't Come Back* (with Ken Gire)
*The Worth of a Man* (with C. W. Neal)
*The Worth of a Man audio*
**Resources by Jan Dravecky**
*A Joy I'd Never Known* (with Connie Neal)
*A Joy I'd Never Known audio*
**Resources by Dave and Jan Dravecky**
*Do Not Lose Heart* (with Steve Halliday)
*Stand by Me* (with Amanda Sorenson)

# Glimpses of Heaven

## Reflections on Your Eternal Hope

### Dave & Jan Dravecky
#### with Amanda Sorenson

Zondervan Publishing House
*Grand Rapids, Michigan*

*A Division of HarperCollinsPublishers*

*Glimpses of Heaven*
Copyright © 1998 by David and Janice Dravecky

Requests for information should be addressed to:

 ZondervanPublishingHouse
*Grand Rapids, Michigan 49530*

---

**Library of Congress Cataloging-in-Publication Data**
Dravecky, Dave.
      Glimpses of heaven : reflections on your eternal hope / Dave and Jan Dravecky ; with Amanda
Sorenson.
        p.  cm.
      Includes bibliographical references.
      ISBN: 0-310-21626-5 (alk. paper)
      1. heaven—Christianity—Quotations, maxims, etc.  I. Dravecky, Jan.  II. Sorenson, Amanda,
1953–   .  III. Title.
      BT844.D74  1998
      236'.24—dc21
                                        98–17624
                                           CIP

---

This edition printed on acid-free paper and meets the American National Standards Institute Z39.48 standard.

Published in association with tthe literary agency of Alive Communications, Inc., 1465 Kelly Johnson Blvd.,
Suite 320, Colorado Springs, CO 80920

All Scripture quotations, unless otherwise indicated, are taken from the *Holy Bible: New International
Version*®. NIV®. Copyright © 1973, 1978, 1984 by International Bible Society. Used by permission of
Zondervan Publishing House. All rights reserved. Scripture taken from the *New American Standard Bible*®
(NASB) © copyright the Lockman Foundation 1960, 1962, 1963, 1968, 1971, 1972, 1973, 1975, 1977, 1995.
Used by permission. Scripture taken from the *New Century Bible* (NCB) used by permission of Word
Publishing, Inc.

*Interior design by Jody DeNeef*

*Printed in the United States of America*

---

98 99 00 01 02 03 04 /✤ DC/ 10 9 8 7 6 5 4 3 2 1

# CONTENTS

Dedicated to the memory of our friend,

Rachel Earll,

Wife of Steve and mother of Emily and Kaylee.

Rachel went to her eternal home in heaven

on August 18, 1997

Approximately eight days before Rachel died, I visited with her for two hours. Her battle with cancer began in 1991, and it was evident as we talked that summer day that her fight was nearing its end. She shared with me her faith and her fears. I listened in awe as I saw her faith in action. I was there to encourage her, but she encouraged me.

Before I left her bedside, I felt led to ask her one last question: "Rachel, what is it that God is saying and showing you at this time?"

She replied, "First, God has shown me that the only thing that matters in life is the Father, the Son, and the Holy Spirit. Second, I am a dying Christian woman. I know I am going to heaven, but I know almost nothing about it. We need to know about where we are going. We need to start teaching about heaven and looking forward to the place that will be our home for eternity."

I left Rachel's bedside with a renewed conviction to share the truth about heaven. So Rachel, this is our answer to your request. It is our feeble attempt to prepare others for heaven, to give them a glimpse of our eternal home.

JAN DRAVECKY

The Lord is my shepherd, I shall not be in want.
He makes me lie down in green pastures,
he leads me beside quiet waters,

he restores my soul.
He guides me in paths of righteousness
for his name's sake.

Even though I walk
through the valley of the shadow of death,
I will fear no evil, for you are with me;
your rod and your staff, they comfort me.

You prepare a table before me
in the presence of my enemies.
You anoint my head with oil; my cup overflows.

Surely goodness and love will follow me
all the days of my life,
and I will dwell in the house of the Lord forever.

PSALM 23

# INTRODUCTION

The familiarity of this oft-quoted Psalm can mask the wondrous truth that God is our loving, faithful shepherd. Through our personal experience in dealing with cancer and through the experiences of hundreds of others who have walked through the valley of the shadow of death, we can testify that the Lord is truly our shepherd.

He will shepherd us through the darkest hours of life, and His greatest desire is to lead each one of us safely to His eternal home in heaven.

Heaven sometimes seems very far away, sometimes not even quite real. But heaven is real. We can count on it. And when we are in the midst of suffering, the hope of heaven can greatly comfort us.

Our desire is to give you a glimpse of heaven, to lift your focus heavenward, to assure you that those who are God's children will indeed live in His house forever. So come, discover the shepherd and the awesome pastures He has prepared for you.

DAVE AND JAN

# HEAVEN IS A LONGING deep within Our Hearts

✳

Whence this pleasing hope, this fond desire,
  This longing for immortality?
  'Tis the divinity that stirs within us;
  'Tis heaven itself that points out an hereafter,
  And intimates eternity to man.

JOSEPH ADDISON

Something deep within us tells us that death is not natural. We fight against it as if it is a foreign enemy, and in a sense it is. God has placed eternity into the heart of every person, so we long for life to go on, yet we are so attached to life on earth that we resist heaven, the true home Jesus has prepared for us.

DAVE DRAVECKY

$\mathcal{H}$e has made everything
beautiful in its time.
He has also set eternity in the
hearts of men; yet they cannot fathom what God has
done from beginning to end.

ECCLESIASTES 3:11

13

We pilgrims walk the tightrope between earth and heaven, feeling trapped in time, yet with eternity beating in our hearts. Our unsatisfied sense of exile is not to be solved or fixed while here on earth. Our pain and longings make sure we will never be content, and that's good: it is to our benefit that we do not grow comfortable in a world destined for decay.

JONI EARECKSON TADA

*I* may not long for death,
but I surely long for heaven.

JOSEPH BAYLY

*I*f I find in myself a desire which no experience in this world can satisfy, the most probable explanation is that I was made for another world.

C. S. LEWIS

They were longing for a better country—a heavenly one. Therefore God is not ashamed to be called their God, for he has prepared a city for them.

HEBREWS 11:16

When we finally realize that the hopes we have cherished will never come true, that a loved one is gone from this life forever, that a child's diagnosis of inoperable cancer will never change, or that we will never be as successful as we had once imagined, our sights are lifted heavenward.

JONI EARECKSON TADA

You guide me with your counsel, and afterward you will take me into glory. Whom have I in heaven but you? And earth has nothing I desire besides you.

PSALM 73:24-25

# ANOTHER TIME, ANOTHER PLACE

I've always heard there is a land
Beyond the mortal dreams of man
Where every tear will be left behind
But it must be in another time

There'll be an everlasting light
Shining a purest holy white
And every fear will be erased
But it must be in another place

(Chorus)
So I'm waiting for another time and another place
Where all my hopes and dreams will be captured
   with one look at Jesus' face
Oh, my heart's been burnin'
My soul keeps yearnin'

Sometimes I can't hardly wait
For that sweet, sweet someday
When I'll be swept away
To another time and another place

I've grown so tired of earthly things
They promise peace but furnish pain
All of life's sweetest joys combined
Could never match those in another time

And though I've put my trust in Christ
And felt His Spirit move in my life
I know it's truly just a taste
Of His glory in another place.

GARY DRISKELL

HEAVEN IS GOD'S HOME,
AND HE WANTS TO SHARE
IT WITH US

✴

For God did not appoint us to suffer wrath but to receive salvation through our Lord Jesus Christ. He died for us so that ... we may live together with him.

1 THESSALONIANS 5:9-10

The LORD has established his throne in heaven, and his kingdom rules over all.

PSALM 103:19

From heaven the LORD looks down and sees all mankind; from his dwelling place he watches all who live on earth.

PSALM 33:13-14

We are not told in the Scripture where heaven is. Nor does it matter. It will be heaven and Christ will be there to welcome us home.

BILLY GRAHAM

Do not let your hearts be troubled. Trust in God; trust also in me. In my Father's house are many rooms; if it were not so, I would have told you. I am going there to prepare a place for you. And if I go and prepare a place for you, I will come back and take you to be with me that you also may be where I am.

THE WORDS OF JESUS AS RECORDED IN JOHN 14:1–3

The chief feature of the New Jerusalem [heaven] is the immediate presence of God. God is in the midst of His people. He dwells with them. No longer is God seen as distant, remote from everyday experience. He pitches His tent in the midst of His people.

R. C. SPROUL

$\mathcal{I}$ heard a loud voice from the throne [in heaven] saying, "Now the dwelling of God is with men, and he will live with them. They will be his people, and God himself will be with them and be their God."

REVELATION 21:3

We have recently walked to heaven's door and put our son's hand into the Lord's hand. Before he went home to be with Jesus, Adam told his tutor that he was in a win-win situation. He said, "If God heals me, I'll be able to ride my bike and I win. If I die, I'll be with Jesus and I win. I win either way."

Yes, Adam won. Even though we miss him more than we can say, we know that just as we showed him the beauty of God's creation on earth, Adam some-day will show us the place God has prepared for us.

JON AND BARB GUSTAFSON

Then the King will say to those on His right,
"Come, you who are blessed of My Father, inherit
the kingdom prepared for you from the foundation of
the world."

MATTHEW 25:34 (NASB)

Our Father refreshes us on the journey with some pleasant inns, but will not encourage us to mistake them for home.

C. S. LEWIS

Our homeland is in heaven, and
we are waiting for our Savior,
the Lord Jesus Christ, to come from
heaven.

PHILIPPIANS 3:20 (NCV)

# SHEER JOY

Oh the sheer joy of it!
Living with Thee,
God of the universe,
Lord of a tree,
Maker of mountains,
Lover of me!

Oh the sheer joy of it!
Breathing thy air;
Morning is dawning,
Gone every care,
All the world's singing,
"God's everywhere."

Oh the sheer joy of it!
Walking with Thee,
Out on the hilltop,
Down by the sea,

Life is so wonderful,
Life is so free.

Oh the sheer joy of it!
Working with God,
Running His errands,
Waiting His nod,
Building His heaven,
On common sod.

Oh the sheer joy of it!
Ever to be
Living in glory,
Living with Thee,
Lord of tomorrow,
Lover of me.

RALPH SPAULDING CUSHMAN

# HEAVEN IS SO AMAZING WE ARE INCAPABLE OF ENVISIONING WHAT IT WILL BE LIKE

It is virtually beyond our power to conceive of a future as consistently delightful as that which Christ is preparing for us. And who is to say what is possible with God?

A.W. TOZER

But as it is written in the Scriptures:
"No one has ever seen this.
No one has ever heard about it.
No one has ever imagined
what God has prepared for those
who love him."

1 CORINTHIANS 2:9 (NCV)

If God hath made this world so fair
Where sin and death abound,
How beautiful beyond compare
Will paradise be found.

JAMES MONTGOMERY

# HEAVEN

Heaven cannot be described
in words of mortal men.
Although the artists do their best,
it can't be drawn in pen.
Imaginations, though they try,
fall short in every way.
For only God can make a place
where all will long to stay.

CARLA MUIR

Revelation reveals only what
we should know for now.
There are some mysteries that God
will leave for us to discover when
we arrive in Paradise.

DAVID JEREMIAH

The description of heaven ... is beyond understanding ... a place so beautiful that when John,
the apostle, caught a glimpse of it, the only thing to
which he could liken it was a young woman on the
crowning day of her life; her wedding day.

BILLY GRAHAM

I saw the Holy City, the new Jerusalem, coming
down out of heaven from God, prepared as a bride
beautifully dressed for her husband.

REVELATION 21:2

A little girl was taking a walk with her father one evening. Looking up at the stars she exclaimed, "O Daddy, if the wrong side of heaven is so beautiful, what must the right side be!"

BILLY GRAHAM

The first lesson we learn about heaven is that life in heaven is better than life on earth.

R. C. SPROUL

Heaven is so peaceful that the storms of earth are there unknown, the stirrings of the flesh are never felt, and the howlings of the dog of hell are never heard. There all is peace and purity, perfection and security forever.

CHARLES HADDON SPURGEON

Let's not get too settled in, too satisfied with the good things down here on earth. They are only the tinkling sounds of the orchestra warming up. The real song is about to break into a heavenly symphony, and its prelude is only a few moments away.

JONI EARECKSON TADA

The history of man has been a continuous series of half successes and total failures. Prosperity exists for a time, only to be followed by war and depression. Twenty-six civilizations have come and gone, and man still battles with the same problems, over and over again.

But the kingdom of God will abide forever. The fluctuations of time, the swinging of the pendulum from war to peace, from starvation to plenty, from chaos to order, will end forever. The Bible says, "And of his kingdom there shall be no end" (Luke 1:33).

BILLY GRAHAM

# Kids' Views of Heaven

God says that heaven is perfect for everyone, and we each have our own idea of what perfect is. My dad died, so part of my perfect heaven would be to have my dad there with me. Best of all, we could see God whenever we wanted.

TAYLOR ANDREWS, AGE THIRTEEN

Heaven will be like living in the clouds with Christ and you can rollerblade on streets of gold. Peter will give you fishing lessons. We'll all be able to fly. We'll play tag in the sky. The trees will be made of gold and the leaves of silver. My point is, heaven is going to be wonderful!

ISAAC ALLEN JONES, AGE ELEVEN

Heaven is a place where you can just have fun. It's a place where you can see your friends again. I'll be happy. I'll be able to put unpleasant times, bad days, seizure medicine . . . all that stuff behind me.

BENJAMIN LEAKE, AGE TEN

*I* think heaven would have blueberries and gold in it. David who fighted Goliath would be there too. Old people will be there and God's angels. There also will be a big, big feast that keeps everybody full.

ANDREW EDWARDS, AGE THREE

*H*eaven will be a place with no sin and no worries, a place with no problems and no hurries.

MEGHAN KALMUS, AGE FIFTEEN

*T*here is no sadness in heaven. There are big houses for the people in heaven that are all equal, so nobody feels better than someone else and no one is jealous.

CAITLIN SORENSON, AGE TEN

HEAVEN IS A REAL PLACE,
AND WE HAVE BEEN GIVEN A
GLIMPSE OF ITS SPLENDOR

The vivid descriptions in Revelation clearly point to a place of utter felicity that is filled with the radiant majesty and glory of God. The inhabitants of the city, God's people, have been sanctified and true justice reigns. Disease, hatred, sickness, and sorrow are banished from the City of God. The extensive visual image gives us just a glimpse of all that God has prepared, giving us a taste of goodness which is more than enough to get us started in desiring to be there.

R. C. Sproul

*H*eaven is not simply a dream
to retreat to when things
get messy and inhospitable on earth.
Heaven is not fantasy.

Eugene H. Peterson

When we as Christians die, we go straight into the presence of Christ, straight to that place, straight to that mansion in heaven to spend eternity with God. We are simply changing our address, much as we would if we moved to another place here on earth. If the post office was capable of delivering the mail in heaven, we could fill out a change of address form because the place we are going to has an address just as the place in which we are now living has an address. It is a real place.

BILLY GRAHAM

And he carried me away in the Spirit to a mountain great and high, and showed me the Holy City, Jerusalem, coming down out of heaven from God. It shone with the glory of God, and its brilliance was like that of a very precious jewel, like a jasper, clear as crystal. It had a great, high wall with twelve gates, and with twelve angels at the gates. On the gates were written the names of the twelve tribes of Israel. There were three gates on the east, three on the north, three on the south and three on the west. The wall of the city had twelve foundations, and on them were the names of the twelve apostles of the Lamb.

REVELATION 21:10–14

The foundations of the city walls were decorated with every kind of precious stone. The first foundation was jasper, the second sapphire, the third chalcedony, the fourth emerald, the fifth sardonyx, the sixth carnelian, the seventh chrysolite, the eighth beryl, the ninth topaz, the tenth chrysoprase, the eleventh jacinth, and the twelfth amethyst. The twelve gates were twelve pearls, each gate made of a single pearl. The great street of the city was of pure gold, like transparent glass.

REVELATION 21:19–21

The angel who talked with me had a measuring rod of gold to measure the city, its gates and its walls. The city was laid out like a square, as long as it was wide. He measured the city with the rod and found it to be 12,000 stadia in length, and as wide and high as it is long. He measured its wall and it was 144 cubits thick, by man's measurement, which the angel was using. The wall was made of jasper, and the city of pure gold, as pure as glass.

REVELATION 21:15–18

The dimensions of the New Jerusalem are 12,000 furlongs, or approximately 1,500 miles broad, wide, and high. The dazzling city's measurements reveal what appears to be a solid cube of golden construction. This could mean 2,250,000 square miles on each tier of the cube, extending 1,500 miles upward like a huge skyscraper . . . . In comparison, the city of London is 117 miles square and contains within it a population of 3.5 million. If we took that same density and moved it into the New Jerusalem, the area would be 1,900,000 square miles. On the basis of the density of London, we can figure that the New Jerusalem could accommodate as many as 53 billion people.

JACK MACARTHUR

There is a river whose streams make glad the city of God, the holy place where the Most High dwells.

PSALM 46:4

Then the angel showed me the river of the water of life, as clear as crystal, flowing from the throne of God and of the Lamb down the middle of the great street of the city. On each side of the river stood the tree of life, bearing twelve crops of fruit, yielding its fruit every month.

REVELATION 22:1–2

Heaven is an affirmation and confirmation that the beauties and sanctities of the visible creation—tree and rock, Jesus and Eucharist—are not illusions that trick us into what cynics think of as the naive, useless, and silly practices of love, hope and faith, but are realities that are in strict correspondence with what has been begun in us and will be complete in us.

EUGENE H. PETERSON

$I$ did not see a temple in the city, because the Lord God Almighty and the Lamb are its temple.

REVELATION 21:22

The city does not need the sun or the moon to shine on it, for the glory of God gives it light, and the Lamb is its lamp. The nations will walk by its light, and the kings of the earth will bring their splendor into it. On no day will its gates ever be shut, for there will be no night there.

REVELATION 21:23–25

The striking visual features of heaven are its symmetry, its light, and its fertility. It is perfectly proportioned, it is light-filled, and it is life-producing. The symmetry is a realization of entire holiness . . . to give us a feel for the enormous wholeness, the vast holiness that reduces every desecration and blasphemy around us to puniness. Everything is proportionate to everything else. Nothing is awkward. Balance, harmony, proportion prevail. Everything fits. Nothing is out of place.

EUGENE H. PETERSON

EVERYTHING IN HEAVEN WILL
BE MADE NEW AND PERFECT

✴

Then I saw a new heaven and a new earth, for the first heaven and the first earth had passed away. . . . And I heard a loud voice from the throne saying . . . "He [God] will wipe every tear from their eyes. There will be no more death or mourning or crying or pain, for the old order of things has passed away." He who was seated on the throne said, "I am making everything new!" Then he said, "Write this down, for these words are trustworthy and true."

REVELATION 21:1, 3–5

We shall be perfect, altogether perfect. This is our hope—victory over evil and perfection in all that is good. . . . As there will be no evil in us, so there will be none around us or about us to cause us alarm. No temporal evil such as pain, bereavement, sorrow, labor, or reproach shall come near us. All will be security, peace, rest, and enjoyment.

CHARLES HADDON SPURGEON

Living in heaven will be a new experience compared to living here on earth. In this world, toys break, kids say mean things, accidents happen, and just about anything that can go wrong, does go wrong. Heaven will be completely different. In heaven, Jesus says, "I'm making everything new." That means we will have a brand-new life in heaven. Jesus has new experiences, new adventures, and special times with him awaiting us in heaven.

JOEY O'CONNOR

Notice how John describes the saints of God in heaven: "they are before the throne of God. They worship God day and night in his temple. And the One who sits on the throne will protect them. Those people will never be hungry again. They will never be thirsty again. The sun will not hurt them. No heat will burn them. For The Lamb at the center of the throne will be their shepherd. He will lead them to springs of water that give life. And God will wipe away every tear from their eyes."

REVELATION 7:15–17 (NCV)

*W*here in all this world
could we turn to find
anything as beautiful, as powerful,
as overwhelming as this description
of the overcoming saints of God
in heaven?

A.W. TOZER

We who are in Christ will be given new and perfect bodies by God in eternity, and He is not dependent on the elements of our old bodies to accomplish this miracle.

BILLY GRAHAM

So I rejoice, and I am glad. Even my body has hope ... because you will not leave me in the grave. You will not let your holy one rot. ... Being with you will fill me with joy. At your right hand I will find pleasure forever.

PSALM 16:9–11 (NCV)

The new body that we will have will be a glorious body like the body of Christ. It will be an eternal body. It will never know tears, heartache, tragedy, disease, suffering, death, or fatigue. It will be a renewed body, but still recognizable.

BILLY GRAHAM

The body that is sown is perishable, it is raised imperishable; it is sown in dishonor, it is raised in glory; it is sown in weakness, it is raised in power; it is sown a natural body, it is raised a spiritual body.

1 CORINTHIANS 15:42-44

There is little or no doubt that personal recognition will be a hallmark of heaven. It is true that there is a strong element of discontinuity between this life and the life to come . . . yet there is a strong element of continuity of the person into eternity. . . . the implication is strong that we will know each other in heaven.

R. C. Sproul

We will recognize our loved ones in Heaven, and they will recognize us. Furthermore, the Bible indicates that we will know them in a far deeper and closer way than was ever possible on earth—and without the imperfections and sins that mar our human relationships on earth.

BILLY GRAHAM

# HEAVEN IS A HOLY PLACE, RESERVED FOR THE RIGHTEOUS

But in keeping with his promise we are looking forward to a new heaven and a new earth, the home of righteousness.

2 PETER 3:13

God has promised a new order [heaven] that will be of eternal duration and infused with eternal life . . . based upon the qualities the exact opposite of mankind's universal blight—temporality and mortality. God promises the qualities of perfection and eternity—qualities that cannot now be found anywhere on this earth.

What a prospect!

A. W. TOZER

Can you imagine a holy city? It would be a community where no one lied, no shady business deals were ever discussed, no unclean movies or pictures were seen. The New Jerusalem will be holy because everyone in it will be holy. Whatever discouraging or dark thoughts enter our minds today will be erased.

DAVID JEREMIAH

The promise of God spoken to John when the wonders of heaven were revealed to him: "It is done. I am the Alpha and the Omega, the Beginning and the End. To him who is thirsty I will give to drink without cost from the spring of the water of life. He who overcomes will inherit all this, and I will be his God and he will be my son."

REVELATION 21:6-7

Nothing impure will ever enter it [the holy city of heaven], nor will anyone who does what is shameful or deceitful, but only those whose names are written in the Lamb's book of life.

REVELATION 21:27

For of this you can be sure: No immoral, impure or greedy person . . . has any inheritance in the kingdom of Christ and of God. Let no one deceive you with empty words, for because of such things God's wrath comes on those who are disobedient.

EPHESIANS 5:5-6

But those who are cowards, who refuse to believe, who do evil things, who kill, who sin sexually, who do evil magic, who worship idols, and who tell lies—all these will have a place in the lake of burning sulfur. This is the second death.

REVELATION 21:8 (NCV)

JESUS CAME TO REVEAL
THE TRUTH. HE DEFEATED DEATH
AND OPENED HEAVEN'S GATES.

We are not left to guess or grope around for the truth—because God has shown us the truth. The Bible tells us something that is almost beyond our comprehension: God himself has come down and walked on the planet . . . died on the cross as a sacrifice for our sins, and He rose again to show us we can be forgiven and can have eternal life with God in Heaven.

BILLY GRAHAM

I tell you the truth, whoever hears my word and believes him who sent me has eternal life and will not be condemned; he has crossed over from death to life. I tell you the truth, a time is coming and has now come when the dead will hear the voice of the Son of God and those who hear will live.

THE WORDS OF JESUS RECORDED IN JOHN 5:24–25

For God so loved the world that he gave his one and only Son, that whoever believes in him shall not perish but have eternal life.

THE WORDS OF JESUS RECORDED IN JOHN 3:16

While there is a great attraction to the idea that "nice" people will go to heaven, Scripture clearly states that all humanity is under penalty of death because of sin. The only way to avoid this penalty and to be given access to God's kingdom is to repent of all sin and accept the cleansing provided through Jesus Christ's death on the cross.

R. C. Sproul

And this is the testimony: God has given us eternal life, and this life is in his Son. He who has the Son has life; he who does not have the Son of God does not have life. I write these things to you who believe in the name of the Son of God so that you may know that you have eternal life.

1 JOHN 5:11-13

Jesus saw people enslaved by their fear of a cheap power. He explained that the river of death was nothing to fear. The people wouldn't believe him. He touched a boy and called him back to life. The followers were still unconvinced. He whispered life into the dead body of a girl. The people were still cynical. He let a dead man spend four days in a grave and then called him out. Is that enough? Apparently not. For it was necessary for him to enter the river, to submerge himself in the water of death before people would believe that death had been conquered.

MAX LUCADO

Since the children have flesh and blood, he too shared in their humanity so that by his death he might destroy him who holds the power of death— that is, the devil—and free those who all their lives were held in slavery by their fear of death.

HEBREWS 2:14–15

$I$ am the Living One; I was dead, and behold I am alive for ever and ever!

THE WORDS OF JESUS RECORDED
IN REVELATION 1:18

For what I received I passed on to you as of first importance: that Christ died for our sins according to the Scriptures, that he was buried, that he was raised on the third day according to the Scriptures, and that he appeared to Peter, and then to the Twelve. After that, he appeared to more than five hundred of the brothers at the same time, most of whom are still living, though some have fallen asleep. Then he appeared to James, then to all the apostles, and last of all he appeared to me.

THE TESTIMONY OF THE APOSTLE PAUL
IN 1 CORINTHIANS 15:3–8

*C*hrist's grave was the birthplace of an indestructible belief that death is vanquished and there is life eternal.

ADOLPH HARNACK

It was not shown to us until our Savior Christ Jesus came. Jesus destroyed death. And through the Good News, he showed us the way to have life that cannot be destroyed.

2 TIMOTHY 1:10 (NCV)

THOSE WHO BELIEVE IN JESUS
NEED NOT FEAR DEATH
FOR THEY, TOO, WILL RISE
TO LIVE AGAIN!

Death is not the end of the road—it is merely a gateway to eternal life beyond the grave. . . . How do I know death is not the end? I know it because Jesus Christ came back from the grave. His resurrection demonstrated once for all that there *is* life after death, and it also demonstrated that He alone can save us and bring us to Heaven.

BILLY GRAHAM

Death comes to everyone because of what one man
did. But the rising from death also happens
because of one man.

1 Corinthians 15:21 (NCV)

Because Christ arose, those who are in Him will
also be raised from corruption to incorruption,
from weakness to power. As a result of this sharing in
His victory, the terrible sting of death is removed and
we have the assurance that our mortality will put on
immortality.

R. C. Sproul

When the perishable has been clothed with the imperishable, and the mortal with immortality, then the saying that is written will come true: "Death has been swallowed up in victory."

"Where, O death, is your victory? Where, O death, is your sting?" . . . But thanks be to God! He gives us the victory through our Lord Jesus Christ.

1 CORINTHIANS 15:54–57

For my Father's will is that everyone who looks to the Son and believes in him shall have eternal life, and I will raise him up at the last day.

THE WORDS OF JESUS RECORDED IN JOHN 6:40

But someone may ask, "How are the dead raised? What kind of body will they have?" Those are stupid questions. When you plant something, it must die in the ground before it can live and grow. And when you plant it, what you plant does not have the same "body" that it will have later. What you plant is only a seed, maybe wheat or something else. But God gives it a body that he has planned for it. And God gives each kind of seed its own body. All things made of flesh are not the same kinds of flesh: People have one kind of flesh, animals have another, birds have another kind, and fish have another. . . . The body that is "planted" will ruin and decay. But that body is raised to a life that cannot be destroyed.

1 CORINTHIANS 15:35–42 (NCV)

Dear friends, now we are children of God, and what we will be has not yet been made known. But we know that when he appears, we shall be like him, for we shall see him as he is.

1 JOHN 3:2

If there is a natural body, there is also a spiritual body. So it is written: "The first man Adam became a living being"; the last Adam [Jesus], a life-giving spirit. The spiritual did not come first, but the natural, and after that the spiritual. The first man was of the dust of the earth, the second man from heaven. As was the earthly man, so are those who are of the earth; and as is the man from heaven, so also are those who are of heaven. And just as we have borne the likeness of the earthly man, so shall we bear the likeness of the man from heaven.

1 CORINTHIANS 15:44–49

Death. The bully on the block of life. He catches you in the alley. He taunts you on the playground. He badgers you on the way home: "You, too, will die someday...."

"Your time is coming," he jabs....

"Everyone has a number," he reminds....

He'll make your stomach tighten. He'll leave you wide-eyed and flat-footed. He'll fence you in with fear. He'll steal the joy of your youth and the peace of your final years. And if he achieves what he sets out to do, he'll make you so afraid of dying that you never learn to live.

That is why you should never face him alone. The bully is too big for you to fight by yourself. That's why you need a big brother....

Jesus unmasked death and exposed him for who he really is—a ninety-eight-pound weakling dressed up in a Charles Atlas suit.... The Christian can face the bully nose-to-nose and claim the promise that echoed in the empty tomb, "My death is not final."

MAX LUCADO

The last enemy to be destroyed will be death.

1 CORINTHIANS 15:26 (NCV)

# IN A SPECIAL LAND

(in loving memory of Karen Larsen)

If I could sit beside you
I would gently hold your hand.
I'd comfort you and tell you of
a very special land.

A land with joy and laughter where
the angels fill the air;
a land of such great beauty that
the Earth cannot compare.

I know in all your sorrow how
you wish me back with you,

though I with life beyond your thoughts
can give you just a view.

So do not put your trust in men
for mortals cannot save.
But put your trust in Jesus Christ
the victor of the grave.

Then whether it is days or years
until I hold your hand—
take comfort, for the Lord and I
are in a special land.

CARLA MUIR

DEATH, DESPITE OUR
FEARS AND PAIN, IS THE
GATEWAY TO HEAVEN

On one hand there is heaven, on the other hand we have to face death to get there. So we wrestle back and forth between the two. . . . Yet the Bible reminds us, "death is the destiny of every man; the living should take this to heart" (Ecclesiastes 7:2). How thankful we can be that death isn't the end!

DAVE DRAVECKY

I remember saying to my dying son, "God won't take you home to be with Him until you're ready."

I then spent a week praying that God would honor those words spoken in love to my eight-year-old son.

During the early morning hours of what came to be Jamie's last day on earth, his breathing became labored. My husband Paul and I knew we were nearing the end. From that moment on, one or both of us was by his side.

It was mid-afternoon when Jamie suddenly looked at the corner of the ceiling and said loudly and clearly, "But I want to stay!" I asked him if he was talking to his father or to me, and he shook his head no. A few hours later, he looked at the same spot in the ceiling and emphatically said, "Go away!" Then he closed his eyes. We were the only visible people in the room, and he was clearly not talking to us.

Later that evening, Jamie shakily lifted both arms off the bed, palms up. Not knowing what was happening, I held him in my arms, and my husband held his hand. Moments later Jamie took his last breath, relaxed, and went home to be with the Lord.

I thank God for letting his father and me be with him when he died. I also thank Him for honoring a promise that a mother made to her son—that God would not take him home until he was ready.

God truly is a God who comforts. I do not pretend to understand His wisdom, nor do I pretend to be happy with His decision to take Jamie home, but I do look forward to being reunited with my son when God takes me to His eternal home.

TINA D'ALESSANDRO

At the hour of death all becomes faith. Faith in God, who knows every fiber of our being and loves us in spite of our sins, is the narrow gate which connects this world with the next.

HENRI J. M. NOUWEN

*Shall I doubt my Father's mercy?*

*Shall I think of death as doom,*

*Or the stepping o'er the threshold*

*To a bigger, brighter room?*

ROBERT FREEMAN

To the majority of people, through most of their lives, death is seen as an enemy, an event to be dreaded because of the traumatic separations and endings it imposes on human life. Once a person comes to realize that death is not final, but is a part of the process, the fear and sorrow is greatly reduced. For the person who suffers and for those who love the sufferer, an understanding of life after death brings great comfort. Death is not just the end of the pain, but is also the release into a new life free of pain.

R. C. SPROUL

Death is . . . deliverance to life beyond your imagining.

JOSEPH BAYLY

Ever since I was a young child, I have believed in Jesus' promise of everlasting life, but the transition called death was always a little scary to me. Watching my son Jamie die with such grace and complete trust removed my fears. I now see death as a short journey. Dying is simply a journey from our life on earth to our eternal home. While I am eager to live, I am also eager to take the journey when God calls me home.

TINA D'ALESSANDRO

Although I want to live and labor as long as God lets me, I consider the moment of my death as the most precious of my life.

FRIEDRICH WILHELM JOSEPH VON SCHELLING

The death incident is merely a passage from earth life, from the womb that has contained you until now, into the marvelous newness of heaven life. You'll go through a dark tunnel, you may experience pain—just as you did when you were born a baby—but beyond the tunnel is heaven. I promise you, you'll enjoy heaven.

JOSEPH BAYLY

Death? Translated into the heavenly tongue, that word means life!

HENRY WARD BEECHER

# WORDS OF THOSE WHO HAVE A HOPE BEYOND THE GRAVE

Our God is the God from whom cometh salvation: God is the Lord by whom we escape death.

MARTIN LUTHER

Earth recedes, heaven opens before me.... this is no dream ... it is beautiful, it is like a trance. If this is death, it is sweet. There is no valley here. God is calling me, and I must go.

D. L. MOODY

The best of all is, God is with us. Farewell! Farewell!

JOHN WESLEY

*I* have been dying for twenty years, now I am going to live.

JAMES DRUMMOND BURNS

*L*ive in Christ, live in Christ, and the flesh need not fear death.

JOHN KNOX

*H*ow different is the epitaph on the tomb of Jesus! It is neither written in gold nor cut in stone. It is spoken by the mouth of an angel and is the exact reverse of what is put on all other tombs: "He is not here: for he is risen, as he said" (Matthew 28:6).

BILLY GRAHAM

# We can safely place our hope in heaven

Praise be to the God and Father of our Lord Jesus Christ! In his great mercy he has given us new birth into a living hope through the resurrection of Jesus Christ from the dead, and into an inheritance that can never perish, spoil or fade—kept in heaven for you, who through faith are shielded by God's power.... In this you greatly rejoice ...

1 PETER 1:3–6

Someday you will read in the papers that D. L. Moody is dead. Don't you believe a word of it. At that moment I shall have gone up higher; that is all; out of this old clay tenement, into a house that is immortal—a body fashioned like unto His glorious body. I was born of the flesh in 1837. I was born of the spirit in 1856. That which is born of the flesh may die. That which is born of the spirit will live forever.

D. L. MOODY

For all can see that wise men die; the foolish and the senseless alike perish. . . . man, despite his riches, does not endure; he is like the beasts that perish. . . . But God will redeem my life from the grave; he will surely take me to himself. Selah.

PSALM 49:10, 12, 15

When we face death, when we face the loss of loved ones, we desperately need a rock-solid hope. The thought that this life is all there is—that we live and then die—is dreadful. When you realize how fragile life is, you search hard for the truth. You have to know what is real. You need a hope beyond this life.

JAN DRAVECKY

We have this hope as an anchor for the soul, firm and secure.

HEBREWS 6:19

I don't know exactly how my thirteen-year-old daughter, Jessica, came to grasp the reality of heaven, but she certainly did. Through her three-and-one-half year struggle with cancer—the horrible chemotherapy, the final weakening stage—her confidence in what lay ahead for her never wavered. I was amazed by how real heaven was to her. I was inspired by her complete peace. I found encouragement in her lack of fear or dread. Our hope, our comfort, and our strength for grieving were immeasurably enhanced by the powerful simplicity of her faith.

I will never forget our last evening with her. She was obviously near death and leaned across my chest. "I'm ready to go now, Daddy," she said.

"Do you mean go to heaven?"

"Yes, Daddy, I'm ready to go over there."

We prayed together one last time, and, surrounded by her family, Jessica slipped peacefully into a coma. A few hours later, God gently took her home.

RON EGGERT

My sheep listen to my voice; I know them, and they follow me. I give them eternal life, and they shall never perish; no one can snatch them out of my hand. My Father, who has given them to me, is greater than all; no one can snatch them out of my Father's hand.

THE WORDS OF JESUS RECORDED IN JOHN 10:27–29

C. S. Lewis was asked by a media interviewer during World War II what he would think if the Germans got the atom bomb, dropped one on England, and he saw it falling right on top of him. "If you only had time for one last thought, what would it be?" Lewis replied that he would look up at the bomb, stick out his tongue at it, and say, "Pooh! You're only a bomb. I'm an immortal soul."

PETER KREEFT

... a faith and knowledge resting on
the hope of eternal life, which God,
who does not lie, promised before the
beginning of time.

Titus 1:2

Cultivate, then, your hope, dearly beloved. Make it to shine so plainly in you that your minister may hear of your hopefulness and joy; cause observers to take note of it because you speak of heaven and act as though you really expected to go there. Make the world know that you have a hope of heaven . . . that you are a believer in eternal glory and that you hope to be where Jesus is.

CHARLES HADDON SPURGEON

No one whose hope is in you
will ever be put to shame.

PSALM 25:3A

There is nothing heroic about our passing, leaving families and friends, but then, death is never heroic and it is never kind. Death is never artistic, always much more likely to be crude and messy and humiliating.

The preacher who once stood with strength and keenness to preach the living Word of God to dying men is now in his bed, his cheeks hollow and his eyes staring, for death is slipping its chilly hand over that earthly tabernacle.

The singer whose gifts have been used to glorify God and to remind men and women of the beauty of heaven above is now hoarse, dry-lipped, whispering only a half-spoken word before death comes.

**But, brethren, this is not the end.** I thank God that I know that this is not all there is. My whole everlasting being, my entire personality—all that I have and all that I am are cast out on the promises of God that there is another chapter!

At the close of every obituary of His believing children, God adds the word *henceforth!* After every biography, God adds the word *henceforth!* There will be a tomorrow and this is the reason for Christian joy.

A.W. TOZER

$S$urely goodness and love will follow me

all the days of my life,

and I will dwell in the house of the LORD forever.

PSALM 23:6

# Dave Dravecky's Outreach of Hope

Therefore we do not lose heart. Though outwardly we are
wasting away, yet inwardly we are being renewed day by
day. For our light and momentary troubles are achieving for
us an eternal glory that far outweighs them all. So we fix
our eyes not on what is seen, but on what is unseen. For
what is seen is temporary, but what is unseen is eternal.

2 Corinthians 4:16–18

On the Sistine Chapel is one of Michaelangelo's most
famous paintings. God is reaching down from heaven
with hand extended to touch the outstretched hand of man.
The natural human response to pain and suffering is often
to do just the opposite—to recoil and retreat. Thus the very
thing we need most, the love and intimacy of God, can
seem furthest from us.

Through Dave and Jan's battles with cancer and
depression, they realized just how necessary love and

encouragement are. At times they experienced the blessing of encouragement—God's touch through the love and actions of people. Their desire is to gently and lovingly pick up the weary arm and lift it heavenward.

To this end they have established Dave Dravecky's Outreach of Hope, a ministry dedicated to offering hope and encouragement through Jesus Christ to those who suffer from cancer or amputation. This mission is accomplished through prayer support, personal contact, correspondence, resource referral, and the gift of encouraging literature. Inquiries may be directed to Dave Dravecky's Outreach of Hope, 13840 Gleneagle Drive, Colorado Springs, CO 80921, or e-mail: info@outreachofhope.org.

# ACKNOWLEDGMENTS

## Heaven Is a Longing Deep Within Our Hearts

Joseph Addison, from Frank S. Mead, 12,000 *Religious Quotations* (Grand Rapids, MI: Baker Book House, reprinted 1989), 224.

Dave Dravecky, *The Encourager* (Spring 1996).

Joni Eareckson Tada, *Heaven . . . Your Real Home* (Grand Rapids: Zondervan Publishing House, 1995), 112. Copyright © 1995 by Joni Eareckson Tada. Used by permission. All rights reserved.

Joseph Bayly, *Heaven* (Elgin, IL: David C. Cook Publishing Co., 1977). Used by permission of ChariotVictor Publishing.

C. S. Lewis, *Mere Christianity* (London: HarperCollinsPublishers). Quote taken from Wayne Martindale and Jerry Root, *The Quotable Lewis* (Tyndale House Publishers), 287. Used by permission of HarperCollinsPublishers. All rights reserved.

Joni Eareckson Tada, *The Encourager.*

Gary Driskell, *Another Time, Another Place.* Words and music by Gary Driskell, copyright © 1990 Word Music, a division of Word Music ASCAP. All rights reserved. Used by permission.

## Heaven Is God's Home

Billy Graham, *Peace with God* (Nashville: Word Publishing, Inc., 1984), 84. Copyright © 1984, Word Publishing, Inc., Nashville, TN. All rights reserved.

R. C. Sproul, *Surprised by Suffering* (Carol Stream, IL: Tyndale House Publishers, 1988). © 1988. Used by permission or Tyndale House Publishers, Inc. All rights reserved.

Jon and Barb Gustafson, *The Encourager.*

C. S. Lewis, *The Problem of Pain* (London: HarperCollinsPublishers, Ltd.). Used by permission of HarperCollinsPublishers. All rights reserved.

Ralph Cushman, "Sheer Joy," poem from *Spiritual Hilltops* (Nashville: Abingdon Press, 1960), taken from Donald T. Kauffman, *The Treasury of Religious Verse* (Fleming H. Revell Co., 1962), 209. Used by permission.

## Heaven Is So Amazing

A. W. Tozer, *Born After Midnight* (Camp Hill, PA: Christian Publications, 1989), 138. Copyright © 1989, Christian Publications. Used by permission. All rights reserved.

James Montgomery, from Frank S. Mead, *12,000 Religious Quotations*, 217.

Carla Muir, "Heaven." Copyright © 1996 by Carla Muir. Used by
    permission.
David Jeremiah, *Escape the Coming Night* (Nashville: Word Publish-
    ing, Inc., 1990), 223. *Escape the Coming Night,* David Jeremiah,
    1990, Word Publishing, Nashville, TN. All rights reserved.
Billy Graham, *Unto the Hills* (Nashville: Word Publishing, Inc.,
    1986), 339, 175. Copyright © 1986, Word Publishing, Inc.,
    Nashville, TN. All rights reserved.
R. C. Sproul, *Surprised by Suffering.* Tyndale House Publishers, 1988.
Charles Haddon Spurgeon, "The Hope Laid Up in Heaven," from
    Warren Wiersbe, *Classic Sermons on Hope* (Grand Rapids, MI:
    Kregel Publications, 1994), 132.
Joni Eareckson Tada, *Heaven . . . Your Real Home,* 16.
Billy Graham, *Unto the Hills,* 324.

## Heaven Is a Real Place

R. C. Sproul, *Surprised by Suffering Study Guide* (Orlando: Ligonier
    Ministries, 1989), 111. © 1989 Ligonier Ministries. Used by
    permission. All rights reserved.
Eugene H. Peterson, *Reversed Thunder* (San Francisco: HarperSan-
    Francisco, 1988), 172. Copyright © 1988 by Eugene H.
    Peterson. Reprinted by permission of HarperCollinsPublish-
    ers, Inc.

Billy Graham, *Unto the Hills*, 60.

Jack MacArthur, *Expositional Commentary on Revelation* (Certain
    Sound Publishing House), 468–69.

Eugene H. Peterson, *Reversed Thunder*, 173.

Eugene H. Peterson, *Reversed Thunder*, 177.


### Everything in Heaven Will Be New and Perfect

Charles Haddon Spurgeon, from Warren Wiersbe, *Classic Sermons
    on Hope*, 131.

Joey O'Connor, *Heaven's Not a Crying Place* (Grand Rapids, MI:
    Fleming H. Revell, 1997), 110. Copyright © by Fleming H.
    Revell, a division of Baker Book House Company. Used
    with permission of the publisher. All rights reserved.

A. W. Tozer, *Jesus Is Victor!* (Camp Hill, PA: Christian Publications,
    1989), 113–14. © 1989, Christian Publications. Used by
    permission. All rights reserved.

Billy Graham, *Answers to Life's Problems* (Nashville: Word Publishing,
    Inc., 1988), 241. Copyright © 1988, Word Publishing, Inc.,
    Nashville, TN. All rights reserved..

Billy Graham, *Peace with God*, 85.

R. C. Sproul, *Surprised by Suffering Study Guide*, 110.

Billy Graham, *Answers to Life's Problems*, 240.

## Heaven Is a Holy Place

A. W. Tozer, *Tragedy in the Church: The Missing Gifts* (Camp Hill, PA: Christian Publications, 1990), 130–31. Copyright © 1990, Christian Publications. Used by permission. All rights reserved.

David Jeremiah, *Escape the Coming Night*, 224.

## Jesus Defeated Death and Opened Heaven's Gates

Billy Graham, *Answers to Life's Problems*, 234.

R. C. Sproul, *Surprised by Suffering Study Guide*, 106–7.

Max Lucado, *Six Hours One Friday* (Sisters, OR: Multnomah Press, 1989), 158. Excerpted from the book *Six Hours One Friday*, by Max Lucado; Multnomah Publishers, Inc., copyright 1989, by Max Lucado.

Adolph Harnack, from George Sweeting, *Who Said That?* (Chicago: Moody Press, 1994), 228.

## Those Who Believe in Jesus Will Rise to Live Again!

Billy Graham, *Answers to Life's Problems*, 236.

R. C. Sproul, *Surprised by Suffering Study Guide*, 104.

Max Lucado, *Six Hours One Friday*, 133–34.

Carla Muir, "In a Special Land." Copyright © 1965 by Carla Muir. Used by permission.

### Death Is the Gateway to Heaven

Dave Dravecky, *The Encourager.*

Henri J. M. Nouwen, *In Memoriam* (Notre Dame, IN: Ave Maria Press, 1980), 31. Copyright © 1980 by Ave Maria Press, Notre Dame, IN 46556. Used with permission of the publisher.

Robert Freeman, from Frank S. Mead, *12,000 Religious Quotations,* 248.

R. C. Sproul, *Surprised by Suffering Study Guide,* 101.

Joseph Bayly, *Heaven.*

Friedrich Wilhelm Joseph von Schelling, from Frank S. Mead, *12,000 Religious Quotations,* 253.

Henry Ward Beecher, from Frank S. Mead, *12,000 Religious Quotations,* 244.

Billy Graham, *Unto the Hills,* 202.

### We Can Safely Place Our Hope in Heaven

D. L. Moody, *Who Said That?* 272.

Jan Dravecky, *The Encourager.*

Ron Eggert, *The Encourager*.

Peter Kreeft, *Blaise Pascal, The Wager* (The Trinity Forum, 1995),
    12. Reprinted from *Christianity for Modern Pagans*, by Peter
    Kreeft, © 1993 Ignatius Press, San Francisco. All rights
    reserved; reproduced with permission of Ignatius Press.

Charles Haddon Spurgeon, from Warren Wiersbe, *Classic Sermons
    on Hope*, 140.

A. W. Tozer, *Who Put Jesus on the Cross?* (Camp Hill, PA: Christian
    Publications, 1975), 85–86. © 1975, Christian Publications.
    Used by permission. All rights reserved.